To Sister Corita Kent and
all the artists like her who have
opened my eyes to new ways
of seeing the world

BEACH LANE BOOKS
An imprint of Simon & Schuster Children's Publishing Division
1230 Avenue of the Americas, New York, New York 10020
© 2021 by Jeanette Winter
Book design by Irene Metaxatos © 2021 by Simon & Schuster, Inc.
All rights reserved, including the right of reproduction in whole or in part in any form.
BEACH LANE BOOKS and colophon are trademarks of Simon & Schuster, Inc.
For information about special discounts for bulk purchases, please contact Simon & Schuster Special Sales
at 1-866-506-1949 or business@simonandschuster.com.
The Simon & Schuster Speakers Bureau can bring authors to your live event. For more information or
to book an event, contact the Simon & Schuster Speakers Bureau at 1-866-248-3049 or visit our website at
www.simonspeakers.com.
The text for this book was set in ITC Avant Garde Gothic Std.
Manufactured in China
0621 SCP
First Edition
10 9 8 7 6 5 4 3 2 1
Library of Congress Cataloging-in-Publication Data
Names: Winter, Jeanette, author, illustrator.
Title: Sister Corita's words and shapes / Jeanette Winter.
Description: First edition. | New York : Beach Lane Books, [2021] | Audience: Ages 3-8 | Audience: Grades 2-3 | Summary: "A
picture book biography of the woman known by some as the Pop Art Nun: Sister Corita Kent, who gained acclaim for her bold,
graphic pop art that calls for peace, equality, and justice"— Provided by publisher.
Identifiers: LCCN 2020046011 (print) | LCCN 2020046012 (ebook) | ISBN 9781534496019 (hardcover) | ISBN 9781534496026
(ebook) • Subjects: LCSH: Corita, 1918–1986—Juvenile literature. | Serigraphers—United States—Biography—Juvenile literature.
| Sisters of the Immaculate Heart of Mary—Biography—Juvenile literature.
Classification: LCC NE2237.5.K4 W56 2021 (print) | LCC NE2237.5.K4 (ebook) | DDC 769.92 [B]—dc23
LC record available at https://lccn.loc.gov/2020046011
LC ebook record available at https://lccn.loc.gov/2020046012

SISTER CORITA'S WORDS and SHAPES

Jeanette Winter

Beach Lane Books

New York London Toronto Sydney New Delhi

Before there was a Sister Corita,
there was Frances Elizabeth Kent,
who lived in Hollywood, and went to the nuns' school,
and drew and painted and painted and drew.

When Frances grew up, she entered
the Immaculate Heart of Mary Convent to become a nun herself.
Frances Elizabeth became Sister Mary Corita.
Corita means "little heart."

Sister Corita is a nun,
and a teacher,
and an artist—
all at the same time.

Behind the windows of the convent
on the hill in Los Angeles,
Sister Corita shows her students a new way of seeing.
She is tiny and moves like a whirlwind.

Her students look at
letters and words and sentences and shapes
and parts of letters and words and shapes
in a different way.

Sister Corita's words tell us what she believes—
she believes in Goodness and in God.

Her days are busy and full,
but Sister Corita's nights are wakeful from insomnia.
Chocolate bars give her daytime energy,
just as her letters and words do.

Sister Corita's letters are BIG or LITTLE
or sideways or upside down or backward.

Her words are LITTLE or BIG
or upside down or sideways or backward.

Her shapes are ALL sizes.

Sister Corita writes words
on the letters or shapes.

She writes her own thoughts
and words from friends and strangers.

The letters and words and shapes and writing are her faith
that she shouts out and shares with the world.

In the city, words are everywhere.

Sister Corita and her students go out to look at
signs, banners, billboards, loaves of bread, boxes of cereal—
EVERYTHING.

They all use a finder to see the details in something BIG.

It's easy to miss a detail in a busy world.

Sister Corita makes silk-screen prints,
remembering details she saw through the finder.

She prints so many copies that
anyone can afford to own one.

St. Mary's Day at the convent, the celebration of the Virgin Mary,
is joyous and colorful and happy.

Just like Sister Corita's prints.

But the archbishop of Los Angeles disapproves.

He likes the old way of worship.

He uses strong words.

He calls Sister Corita's modern ideas blasphemous.

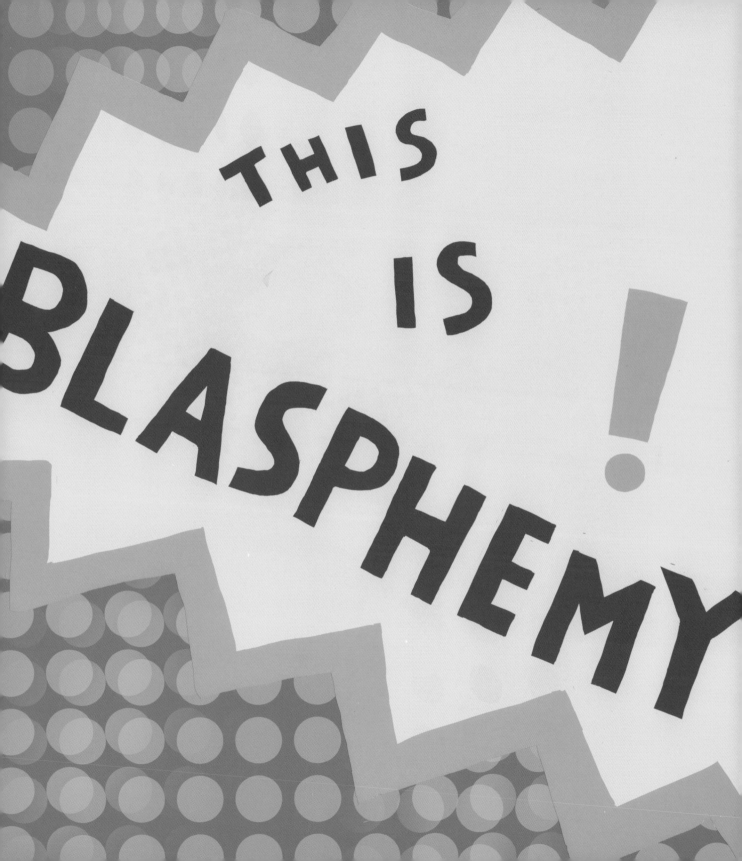

But the sisters and students feel
JOY and LOVE and HAPPINESS

celebrating Mary in this new way.

Life becomes hard for Sister Corita
because of the archbishop's disapproval.
She lies awake at night, still unable to sleep.
"It has all become too much."

So Sister Corita packs her bag
and travels across the country to Boston.
She never returns to Immaculate Heart,
her home for over thirty years.

Sister Corita becomes simply Corita.
She moves into a brownstone with a big bay window
where she sits for hours ...
looking at the maple tree just outside.

By now, Corita and her work are famous.
She is asked to decorate a huge gas tank.
Corita paints little sketches of a rainbow
for the painters to work from.

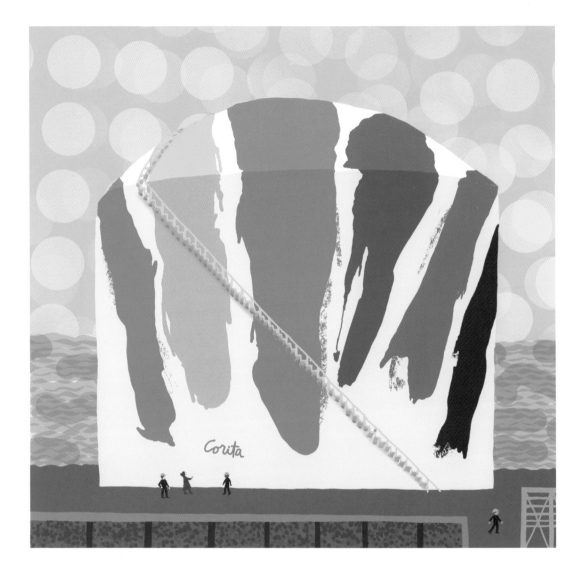

In six weeks, five painters copy Corita's rainbow,
using 555 gallons of paint.
A WONDER!

The promise of the rainbow tank
comes from Corita's dark moments.
"Our job is to make flowers grow."

Corita's billboard is her message of peace
to the city.

Her small stamps send love
into the big world
as she finds peace in her new life.

peace
sand
quiet

Corita left the church, but she never left God.
And God never left Corita.

Now her church is her vision.
Her words are her prayers.
Her art is her life.

"I am trying to make hope."

Sister Corita made a set of rules for her students
at Immaculate Heart College:

10 RULES

RULE 1   Find a place you trust and then try trusting it for a while.

RULE 2   General duties of a student: Pull everything out of your teacher.
Pull everything out of your fellow students.

RULE 3   General duties of a teacher: Pull everything out of your students.

RULE 4   Consider everything an experiment.

RULE 5   Be self-disciplined. This means finding someone wise or smart
and choosing to follow them. To be disciplined is to follow in a
good way. To be self-disciplined is to follow in a better way.

RULE 6   Nothing is a mistake. There's no win and no fail. There's only make.

RULE 7   The only rule is work. If you work it will lead to something.
It's the people who do all of the work all the time who eventually
catch on to things.

RULE 8   Don't try to create and analyze at the same time. They're
different processes.

RULE 9   Be happy whenever you can manage it. Enjoy yourself.
It's lighter than you think.

RULE 10   "We're breaking all of the rules. Even our own rules. And how do
we do that? By leaving plenty of room for X quantities."
—John Cage

Helpful hints: Always be around. Come or go to everything. Always go to
classes. Read anything you can get your hands on. Look at movies carefully,
often. Save everything—it might come in handy later.

There should be new rules next week.

The Artist with Three Names

Frances Elizabeth Kent	Sister Mary Corita	Corita Kent
1918–1936	1936–1968	1968–1986

Corita was very much a part of the political and social causes of the 1960s.

The Vietnam War, the Civil Rights Movement, and pop art informed her work.

In 1962, the Second Vatican Council (Vatican II) brought new ideas of openness and individual freedom to the Catholic Church. The sisters of the Immaculate Heart of Mary embraced Vatican II. Finally they could wear street clothes and be flexible about their daily prayer and traditional worship. In the past, their annual St. Mary's Day, a celebration of the Virgin Mary, had been a day of formal ceremony. But now, under Sister Corita's direction, it became an outdoor event of joy, with sisters and participants adorned with flowers and carrying posters of LOVE, all celebrating together.

Cardinal James Francis McIntyre, archbishop of Los Angeles, was a conservative Catholic. Upset by Sister Corita's changes to St. Mary's Day, he called her art anti-religious and Communist and attacked her for being blasphemous. Soon after, Corita left the order entirely and moved to Boston. Three hundred and fifteen sisters (out of 380) also left the Immaculate Heart of Mary Convent. The sisters continued their work, becoming the Immaculate Heart Community.

While planning and working on this book, I pinned up many postcard images of Corita's prints. Seeing them around me every day was a joyful and inspiring experience. Then in March 2020, COVID-19 descended on New York City. It wasn't until that dark and terrifying time that I felt the full impact of her faith made visible: HOPE.   —J. W.

Selected Bibliography

Ault, Julie. *Come Alive! The Spirited Art of Sister Corita*. London: Four Corners, 2006.

Berry, Ian, and Michel Duncan, eds. *Someday Is Now: The Art of Corita Kent*. New York: Prestel Verlag, 2013.

Kent, Corita. *Footnotes and Headlines: A Play-Pray Book*. New York: Herder and Herder, 1967.

Kent, Corita, and Jan Steward. *Learning by Heart*. New York: Bantam, 1992.

Pacatte, Rose. *Corita Kent: Gentle Revolutionary of the Heart*. Collegeville, MN: Liturgical, 2017.